To James

with love

Alpha

May 1984

HONEY

HONEY

by
Sarah Munro

Illustrated by
Alan Male

FRANKLIN WATTS
London and New York

Franklin Watts Limited
26 Albemarle Street
London W1

Copyright © 1977 Franklin Watts Limited
SBN 85166 625 6

Thanks are due to the International Bee Research
Association, to Manley Ratcliffe Limited and to F. G. Vernon
for permission to reproduce photographs.

Filmset and printed in Great Britain by
BAS Printers Limited, Wallop, Hampshire

For thousands of years people have stolen honey
from the nests of honey bees because of its
delicious **taste** and natural **goodness**.
Honey is rich in different sorts of **sugars** that
give you **energy**.
It contains **vitamins** to keep you **healthy**, and
minerals that help you **grow**.

We use honey in many ways.

First of all, we **eat** it.

We spread it on bread and butter.

We add it to drinks.

We mix it with food instead of sugar.

Many athletes and sportsmen have a spoonful of honey before a race to give them instant energy.

The famous climber **Sir Edmund Hillary**
included honey in his diet during his ascent of
Mount Everest.
He knew the value of honey because
he had often helped out on his father's
large bee-farm in New Zealand.

Scientists recently discovered that certain germs
  cannot live in honey.
It is an **antiseptic** (meaning that it kills germs).
We can put it on cuts and boils to help them
  heal.
We can take it to **soothe** our coughs and sore
  throats.

Honey helps to **soften** the skin, so it is used in
cosmetics, in hand and face creams.
It is smeared inside bagpipes to make the leather
soft and supple.

Not only do people like it.
Bears rob bees' nests, and so do **mice, insects**
and other creatures.

Long ago in Egypt a jar of honey used to be
placed in a **tomb** with the dead as food for
them on their journey to the underworld.
One jar was found in a tomb 3,300 years old.
Drawings of early people putting honey in jars
have been found in caves.

Many early people thought that honey was
either for the **gods**, or a gift from the gods.
They also believed that honey would make
people **immortal** (so that they would never
die).
At sacred festivals in Peru, South America,
honey used to be offered to the **sun god**.

In Italy the Romans, like the Egyptians and
    Greeks before them, used honey for preserving
    fruit.
They also put honey in cakes and drinks.

In Europe until the 1600s, when sugar became cheaper than honey, everyone used honey for **sweetening**.

Honey was also used to give salted meat (salt was used for preserving) a more pleasant taste.

The most famous thing made from honey was **mead**, which was drunk by most people during the Middle Ages.

At first, the only way people could obtain honey without being stung was to **smoke** the bees away from their nest.

Next they learnt how to remove part of the branch or tree trunk where bees had **swarmed** (gathered together) and to take it back to a place near their homes.

There they would keep the bees in **hives**.

When the combs are filled with a lot of honey a swarm of bees may leave the hive and settle together on a bush or tree. This bee-keeper is collecting such a swarm, and he will put the bees into another hive.

hive made of coiled straw

In some tropical countries, the first hives were
mud cylinders and **earthenware pots**.
In Europe hives were made of **bark** or **coiled
straw** and were often coated with honey and
herbs to attract the honey bees into them.

Honey bees can be bought from a bee-keeper.
Or, if bee-keepers are lucky enough to find a
swarm clustered around a tree, the bees can
be captured with the help of a **smoker** and
cost nothing.

**Bee-keepers also use smokers to control bees
when a hive is open. This bee-keeper needs to
puff just a little smoke from the smoker in
her right hand to control the bees.**

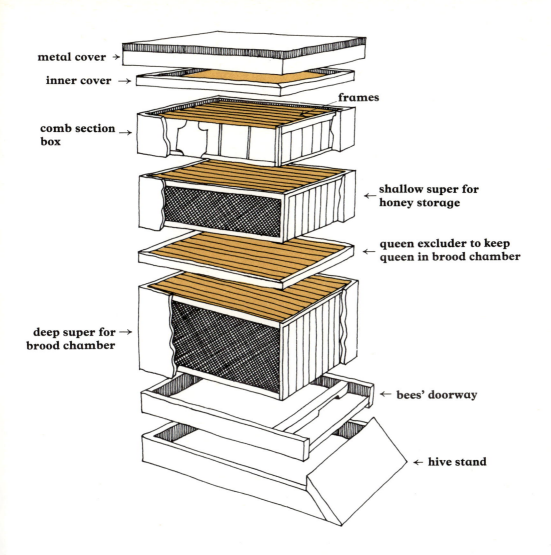

metal cover →

inner cover →

frames

comb section box →

shallow super for honey storage ←

queen excluder to keep queen in brood chamber ←

deep super for brood chamber →

bees' doorway ←

hive stand ←

Here is the inside of a wooden hive used today.
The metal **roof cover** protects the bees from
heat or cold.

The **supers** are chiefly the bees' larders, where
they store honey in individual wooden comb
holders called **frames**.

In a hive there are three sorts of honey bee:
the **queen**, the **drones** and the **workers**.

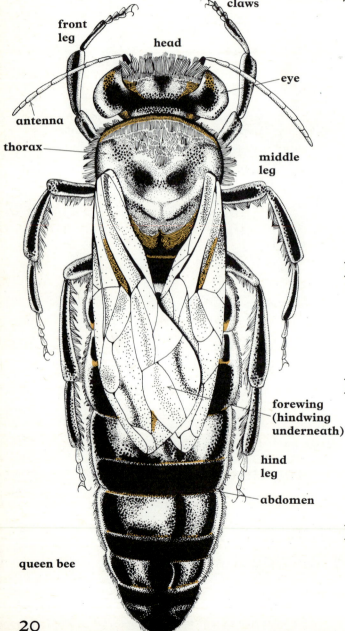

claws

front
leg

head

antenna

thorax

eye

middle
leg

forewing
(hindwing
underneath)

hind
leg

abdomen

queen bee

The **queen-excluder** keeps the queen bee (the most important member of the hive) in the **brood chamber**, where she lays all the eggs for the honey bee colony. From spring to autumn she may lay up to 2000 eggs every day. If the queen is killed or removed from the hive, the bees cannot work properly. In a hive there are about 40,000 workers.

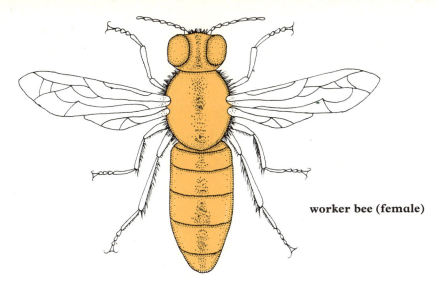

worker bee (female)

It is the workers who make the honey for all the
bees during the summer (honey is bees' food).
They store it for the winter and for cold wet
days when they do not leave the hive.

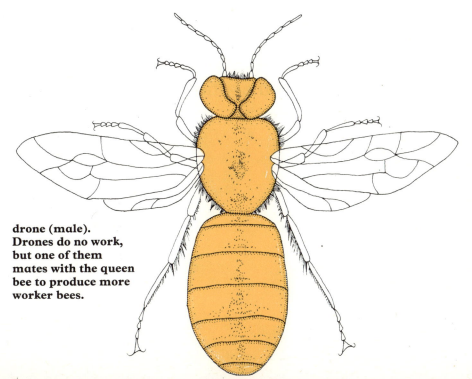

drone (male).
Drones do no work,
but one of them
mates with the queen
bee to produce more
worker bees.

At three weeks' old the worker bee begins her job as a **scout** searching for **nectar**.

Nectar is a sweet liquid made up of sugars and found in the **nectaries**, or honey-bearing parts, of flowers.

As soon as the worker has discovered a mass of flowers with nectar, she returns to the hive and tells the other workers where it is by doing a **honey dance** on the comb.

The **scent** of the flowers on her body, the **direction** in which she dances, and the **speed** of her movements tell the other workers how far and in which direction they must fly to find the nectar.

The scout also gives the other workers samples of the nectar so they know what kind of flowers to look for.

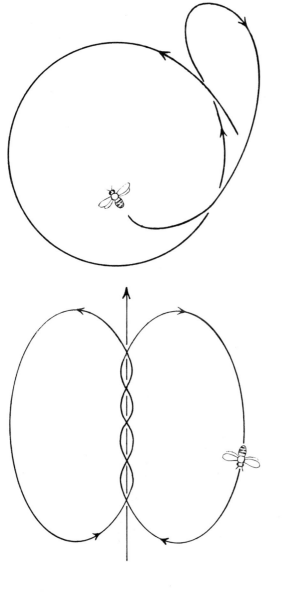

The "round dance" tells other bees that there is food within 10 metres (30 feet)—but gives no direction.

In the "waggle-tail dance" the bee waggles its abdomen during the straight run.
The dotted arrow indicates the direction of the food.
The speed of circling indicates distance—if the bee moves quickly it means food is near by; if it moves more slowly it means food is further away.

These two main "bee dances" were discovered by an Austrian scientist, Karl von Frisch. Other dances vary between these two extremes.

It is the job of the workers to collect the nectar.
When they get to the flowers, they suck the
  nectar up from the nectaries and store it in
  their **honey sacs**.

**Honey bee collecting nectar from white clover,
which gives a delicately-flavoured honey**

Perhaps you have watched the bees at work.
You may have noticed how the bees often prefer
one sort of flower in the garden to another.
The amount of nectar from a flower varies
according to the **temperature** of the day.
For example, white clover needs a temperature
of 21°C (70°F) before it gives out any nectar.

white clover

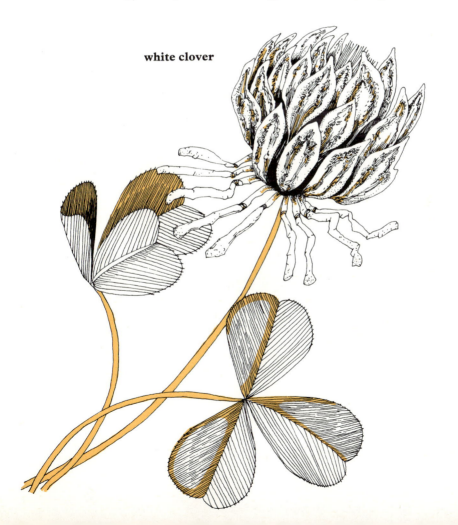

Dry weather affects nectar.

If there has been no rain for a long time, the flow gets less.

The bees then have to collect something called **honeydew**, a sticky sap produced by tiny insects moving on the underside of leaves.

Sometimes we find honeydew all over a car's windscreen if the car has been left beneath certain trees.

Bees will travel only about 4·8 kilometres (3 miles) from their hive.

So if there is little nectar around because most of the flowers near the hive are finished, the bee-keeper may move the hive to where there is more nectar to be found.

If there is no nectar to be had at all, bees will steal it from each other or, perhaps, raid a weaker colony unable to defend itself.

The average amount of honey expected from a hive is between 15–20 kilos (33–44 lbs).

Heather has much nectar so the bee-keeper
might take the hive onto the moors during the
month of August.

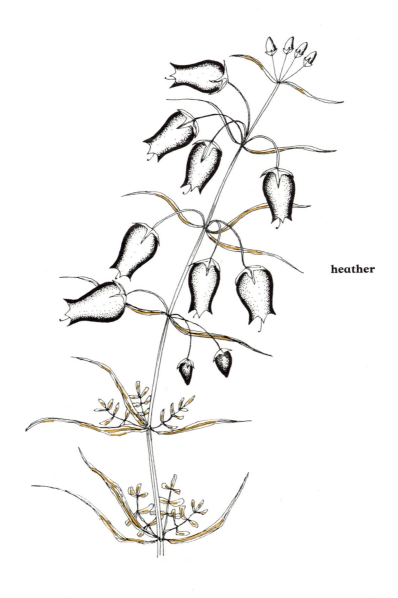

heather

A hundred years ago the French used to put
    their hives on **barges** and move them up and
    down rivers, going from one group of flowers
    on the bank to the next.

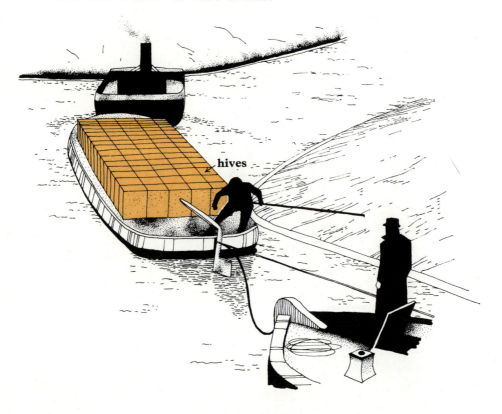

hives

When a worker returns, heavy with nectar,
    to the hive, she passes the nectar to the mouth
    of an indoor working bee who swallows it
    down into *her* honey sac.

This indoor worker then repeatedly pumps the
nectar out and sucks it in, to let the warm air
of the hive get at it and cause it to lose some
of its water.

In this way and by passing the nectar from bee
to bee, the water in the nectar is reduced from
70% to less than 20%.

bees sealing honey in the comb cells

Then the nectar is stored in the **comb cells**. Sometimes it is stored at once in the comb cells (before it goes from mouth to mouth) because the water in the nectar may have been reduced by the heat in the hive.

The journey the nectar makes, together with special substances the worker has in her body called **enzymes**, change the nectar into honey.

However, it has to undergo more changes in the cells before the bees consider it ready to cover and **seal** with a **wax cap**.

Once all the combs in the supers are capped, the
bee-keeper can **collect** the honey.

But to make sure the bees have enough food to
eat during the cold winter months, the bee-
keeper later feeds them with sugar in the form
of **candy** or **syrup**.

bee-keeper removing supers full of combs from the hive

In order not to be stung, the bee-keeper wears
protective clothing: usually a mesh **veil**,
leather **gloves** and an all-in-one **suit**.
First, the bee-keeper clears the bees away from
the supers by placing a special **board** between
the lowest super and the brood chamber.
This allows the bees to descend into the brood
chamber but stops them returning.

Next, when the combs are clear of bees, the bee-
keeper takes the supers out of the hive and
removes them to a workroom.

Here the wax cappings are scraped off with a
hot sharp knife and the combs placed in an
extractor (see picture below).

This machine whirls the uncapped combs round
and round, and flings the honey out of the
wax.

The honey then runs off into a pail below.

The clean combs are then returned to the hive
for the bees to fill up again.

The honey, which has been extracted, is **strained** and allowed to **stand** for a few hours to let the air bubbles come to the top and escape.

Then it is poured into **jars**.

Some of it is allowed to **granulate** (**crystallise** or become **hard**) and some is left **runny**.

(Nearly all honeys granulate sooner or later, because the **glucose** (the sugary substance) in them separates out into **crystals**, thickening and turning a lighter colour.)

But the bee-keeper may not always put the honey comb into an extractor, but may simply cut the comb up into chunks and fill containers with them.

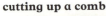

cutting up a comb

section honey

Or, if instead of frames the bee-keeper put four-sided little boxes called **sections** into the hive, he or she will remove them once they are full and use or sell them as they are.

Most of the honey we eat comes from countries where it is very sunny and hot.

Long summers and thousands of flowers allow bees to gather nectar over many months.

In **temperate** (or cooler) countries like Britain there is a short summer and bee-keepers cannot produce enough honey to satisfy everyone.

So people buy honey from countries such as
Australia and from parts of America where
they have special **bee farms**.
In temperate countries there are very few bee
farms.
Bee-keeping is mainly a **hobby**.

Imported honey is shipped in 163 kilogram
(360 lb) drums and sent to **packing plants**.
Most imported honey arrives granulated.
At the packing plants it is examined by experts
who decide whether it should be sold in a
granulated or a runny form.

If some is to be sold as **liquid** (or runny) **honey**, it is heated at a special temperature until it **liquefies**.

Then it is piped through **filters** to remove any wax floating about in it.

filling pots with honey

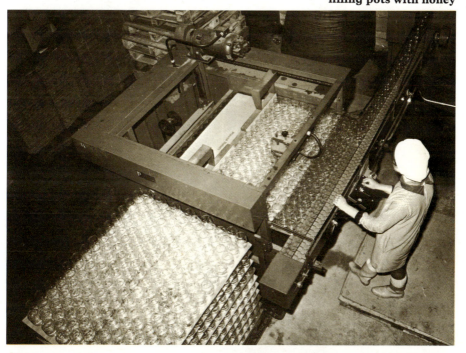

Finally the jars are filled either with honey from **one type** of flower, such as clover, or with honey which is a **mixture** of three different honeys of the same colour.

This makes sure the honey is of the best quality.

You may have noticed in your local supermarket
how many **colours** honey comes in.
Its colour depends on the kind of flower from
which the nectar was gathered.
For the same reason honey tastes differ too.

clover

ling heather

sainfoin   lime

Here are some examples of nectar sources and
the colours of honey they produce.

Country	Flowers	Colour of Honey
In Australia	box and gum trees	pale yellow
In Britain	ling heather	deep golden
	clover	white
	lime	greenish
	sainfoin	lemon

gum tree

box

Country	Flowers	Colour of Honey
In Greece	wild thyme	bright yellow
In Spain	orange blossom	orange
In USA	buckwheat	dark brown

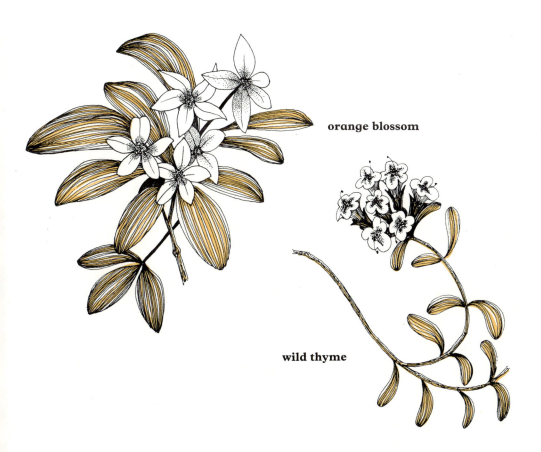

orange blossom

wild thyme

RECIPES USING HONEY

Honey Butter: 100 grammes (4 oz) butter

$\frac{1}{4}$ cup of runny honey

Make sure the butter is at room temperature.

Put it in a bowl and beat it with a wooden
spoon until it is fluffy.

Gradually add the honey and go on beating the
mixture until it is thoroughly blended.

Spread it on hot toast.

Remember: it is easy to take honey from the jar
if you first dip the knife or spoon in hot water.

Honey Milk Shake: 2 cups of milk

2 tablespoons of honey

pinch of cinnamon

pinch of ginger

Whisk all the ingredients hard with a beater for about 2–3 minutes, or put all the ingredients into an electric blender and switch on for a few seconds.

Pour the mixture into a jug and place it in the refrigerator.

(This makes enough for two milk shakes.)

Honey Glazed Baked Apples: apples
honey
cinnamon
cloves
butter
1 cup of hot
water

Peel and core as many cooking apples as needed.
Place them in a baking dish.

Fill their centres with honey, a pinch of
cinnamon, a clove, and top with a knob of
butter.

Make a syrup with a full tablespoon of honey
and the cup of hot water.

Pour the syrup into the baking dish.

Bake at Elec. 180°C (350°F), Gas Mark 4 for
about 45 minutes.

Baste them occasionally.

Honey French Dressing: $\frac{1}{2}$ cup of salad oil
(for a salad) $\frac{1}{2}$ cup of lemon juice
$\frac{1}{2}$ cup of runny honey
$\frac{1}{2}$ teaspoon of salt
pepper
1 clove of garlic—
crushed

Put everything into a jar with a tight lid.
Shake it as hard as you can.

Honeydate Cookies: 225 grammes ($\frac{1}{2}$ lb) raisins
225 grammes ($\frac{1}{2}$ lb) dates
1 cup of honey
1 cup of boiling water

Put all the ingredients into a pan.
Cook them over a low heat, stirring all the time
  with a wooden spoon until the mixture is thick.
Turn it into a greased tin and cut into squares.
Leave to cool.

For coughs and colds: 1 tablespoon of honey
1 tablespoon of lemon
  juice
285 ml ($\frac{1}{2}$ pint) of hot
  water (not boiling or
  the glass will crack)

Put all the ingredients into a glass.
Stir the honey until it is dissolved.
Drink the mixture while it is hot.

Index